limerence

"In Octavio González's first book-length poetry collection, *limerence*, he probes the inextricable tension, pain, pleasure, and danger in relationships with men. As a gay man, who immigrated to the United States from the Dominican Republic, González writes poems that convey an all-consuming, yet ever elusive search for home and place in the intimacy of both fleeting sexual encounters and long-term relationships. In the therapist's office, on rooftops, and in bedrooms, González navigates love, lust, and longing. González's experience of love, sexual desire and romance is not sentimental as these experiences are often intertwined with questions of consent and violence. Poignant and searing, this collection will have the readers both appreciating and reexamining the meaning of love, trust, and safety."   **—Pia Deas**, author of *Cargo*

"In *limerence*, Octavio González gifts us with a lusty archive of what the poet's remembered body tells, keeping readers adrift and glued to the funk of history, longing, and desire. His is a libation to what makes queer bodies burn."

—Carlos Ulises Decena, author of *Tacit Subjects*
and *Circuits of the Sacred*

"Octavio González's inaugural book of poetry, *limerence*—after a crafty stream of bodily excuses—after loosening our attention like a thief, steals all of our belongings ... and we are left naked and free at the beach. Limerence quells the urges and repetitions of reading the concrete and abstract valences of love's passing reality. Like "that shaved part of every boy's neck," there is nothing about it I don't like."

—**Scott Hightower**, author of *Part of the Bargain*
and *Imperative to Spare*

"*limerence* is revelatory, fierce, and filthy in the most profound way. Octavio González is a daring, fresh, exciting, and necessary new voice to our LGBTQ+ and Latinx literary tradition."

—**Emanuel Xavier**, author of *Pier Queen*
and *Christ Like*

"The newest release by Octavio R. González is a tour-de-force introspective offering to the literary world. As has always been my experience with his writing, González has found a way to grab the reader in the first few words, painting intimate and jaggedly imaginative experiences for us all to bask in and at times take pause to reflect on what the narrator is trying to tell us or make us see. A standout poem for me is "rooftop (ii)," a coming-of-age reflection of gay youthful bliss. *limerence*, in all of its glory, stirs up the same ecstatic feelings I had when I first read E. Lynn Harris and Reinaldo Arenas— unfiltered, raw, sexy, beautiful and awakening. This new collection by González is a beautiful contribution to the field, and I am sure we'll all be infatuated with it for years to come."

—**Seth Parker Woods**, creator of *Difficult Grace*

limerence

octavio r. gonzález

QUEERMOJO
A Rebel Satori Imprint
New Orleans

Published in the United States of America by
Rebel Satori Press
www.rebelsatoripress.com

Cover art by Steven Harris

Paperback ISBN: 978-1-60864-252-6
Library of Congress Control Number: 2023930076

first he auctioned off his legs. eyes.
heart. in rooms of specific pain.
he specialized in generalize
learned newyorkese and all profane.
—sonia sanchez

when aunt is dead, her terrified hands will lie
still ringed with ordeals she was mastered by.
the tigers in the panel that she made
will go on prancing, proud and unafraid.
—adrienne rich

i only knew that she was lovable in a way that no human could
ever quite be, since, being a creature of art, she had been
created out of pure love.
—christopher isherwood

limerence:

the state of being romantically infatuated or obsessed with another person, typically experienced involuntarily and characterized by a strong desire for reciprocation of one's feelings but not primarily for a sexual relationship.

—oxford english dictionary

contents

1

when i was little (i)

i was warned not to put change in my mouth or else
i would swallow it. i used to swirl nickels, pennies,
even dimes sometimes ever so gently like treasure.

one time i swallowed a nickel. i
panicked, but my family told me it would be okay. i
looked for it for days after this. i never held coins in
my mouth again, knowing it would not be safe.

2

shrink (i)

he stood 6'4, scandinavian tall,
ben franklin hair. we met in his
pvt office on the upper west
side. i was 15, which he knew and

after he blew, nonchalantly asked
if i wanted to go
sailing with him some time?
but i jump ahead. the climax

came when he pounded my
mouth. it was fucking enormous
which i knew for i'd had average
before

      (the other pederast who
wanted to know where me & my friends
hung out—the mall?)

               i gagged.

kriss kross

two black teen hip-hop stars
ballooned jeans worn backwards
bass thumping while on all fours
getting licked for the first time, boy
hole clenched as the middle-aged
pederast hummed into my ass.

smelled like irish spring, plush white
towel, fresh from the shower he
brushed my lips, timidly

                    at first

                                   jump jump
mtv blared (or was it radio?) as i blanched
from his desire: *give ya something that you
never had   make ya bump, hump, wiggle and
shake your rump:* 15yo prisoned in a
box of teeth, box of words like
i want you to shit in my mouth

shrink (ii)

ben franklin was lean, impossibly
erect, his tongue a snail
sliming across my lips, gunmetal
hair curtained lanky shoulders, rail
thin jeans, flimsy western shirt,
pearl snaps open to the waist:
hippie shrink. i barely half his
height, he four times my age. after that

froggy kiss (drizzle of acid rain)
long gentle fingers flicked
my uncut nail. the hour ended with
him pounding my face, engrossed in
brute geometry, fucked in violent
pantomime, salt jets scalding my throat

the hole in the middle of my heart, called

mine.

       i wanted to say

                but why

                        the fuck don't i

                              just go

out alone

          for a cruisy bit of latenight

      you wonder as you undo
      the fantasy of dancing

                all night long

                      lost in still

life

     tableaux
     without faces

           marching

              molly & k, antennas of sensation

surround

     and beyond

         locating   me

eyes glazed unfocused
swimming in

        sweat

          sounds of

               glory

                   prime
                   time

                         militia

in search of the million-dollar man
with a body of meticulous gold and

               a set of those

                   deep brown

eyes

    of

      course

        but he's right
        here dancing next

to me

    torso exposed like a side
    of pigskin

            and boy do i spin

bubble chest like tits, amazing
how the eye licks meat
                        confusing
                                    appetite for hunger.

drum n bass explosions—technicolor
beams

                screwing my senses into
                                    worlds like this

                        (started at fifteen
when i lingered all
                        afternoon over a tall blond dream

in white polo shirt who
                        desperately
                                    wanted to kiss me
                                                        and
i wanted too)
                in
            memory

                                of that shaved
                                            part of every

boy's neck

       teasing brown eyes

              turning toward me

                      ·   my head

swiveling

     out of sequence

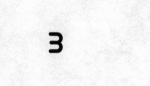

rooftop (i)

we met at brunch in little tokyo. he
was thirtysomething, visiting from miami
(or was it fort lauderdale?) i forget
how we spent sunday into monday
gliding through alphabet city, except
where we ended:
                        on the rooftop
of my shared sublet on 1st avenue. at 19
i still had my anal cherry and
i'd told him i wanted it
to be him: he had a soft face. barely

did i feel him going in—we fucked high as
indigo & crimson tie-dyed summer sky
with no lube, but it was—what

we didn't do with the used rubber, came later.

rooftop (ii)

used rubber nailed to our front door
forgotten in hazy afterglow: getting fucked
for the first time, at dawn, high on
mj and joy.

           the middle-aged white male
couple upstairs found it on the roof—
which they'd gayified, not just for them
selves but us too, and that's how we
behaved?
              (we being 3 twinks
of color on our own.) they won't
look you in the face, my alpha roommate
smirked—as the other silently second-
guessed letting me move in—parading
me to see this soggy display, crucified.
but it was hilarious, so they laughed

as i climbed upstairs to apologize.

baywatch apollo

accidentally, proudly after he's gone:
sweaty neon thighs, saltwater nights
wakened to fogged mornings: tanned '70s
beachboy shag, bronze monterey smile, dirty
blond mustache—amazing how the eye licks
meat, confusing appetite for hunger.

was he herald only to the gaudy spring?
i, corrugated sentinel washed by
union square skies, warding december
games: hopscotch on rainbowed sidewalks,
bland office mates under fluorescent light,
hips locked after hours in the dark.

                              sun king

disassembled: son of man, shaving cream
(scars on my back where my wings used to be)

limerence

scars on my back where my wings used to be
(sometimes, i get goosebumps thinking of him
nourished with what i was consumed by: smudged
ring, yellow shit, warm marble tongue licking
wet garden musky with rosemary and

        hello & goodbye to the boy-man
in matching parachute pants: onion-
paper bags under his eyes, clammy hand
on a bed of seashells, empty with me
in it? strobe lights throbbed in a hazy maze
under the skin. so i began to sing
warbled blue notes meant for him to hear, ringed
lips smoking what could tranquilize, restore

eucharist

lips smoking what could tranquilize, restore
ghosting, silent gestures. yellow lines, green
ink folded over, opened as a christ
mas gift: a new you, with complicated
hands embracing my cold feet, which you swore
to keep warm—forever? what a story,
my telenovela, red-carpet star.

fountain of piss in a dim st. mark's place
motel, drinking rum rain that stained the floor
but the taste (another word for love) was
not 'candied sweet'—was no eucharist. my ex
foretold the scene, and perceived the rest,
glared at the soles of his feet, summoning
the beat to move on. our tangle just began.

magical thinking

moving to the beat, our tango just began:
my own private idaho bronco ride
under mormon white cotton sheets that soon
reddened and bloomed. sprung loose like a baby's
tooth (in spanish we say *milky*), twisting it
back and forth, side to side, because
it hurt so good. because it's time, you say, but

you didn't say. you come out swinging, lip
syncing while i dance in a darkened hall
only to ride shotgun at dawn. green sweat
cooling your brow, bitter blaze of my kohl
eyes, charcoal tongue and bulging
adam's apple stuck in your throat. my lips
blackening with loss, burning like fireflies

cobalt sonata

blackened with loss, lips burn like fireflies.
mami's knocking frantically on my
bedroom door: 'your friend's on the phone,' she
tries. 'she's crying.'

        (nighttime shadow under
low ceiling of bottled stars, shivering indigo
fingers, black & white polished nails
clutching hospital-grade blankets, ice
air. fever dream pirouettes, silhouetted i
tower over sharp skyscrapers.

my friend on the other side of the world's
already gone: cobalt windbreaker,
strawberry scented hair.)

        i wobble from my
childhood bed to unlock the door, saved.

dark stars

i wobble from my childhood bed, saved by a
sad teenage pact between best friends. those
were days of passionate self hate. yes, we
drew sonnets in pencil and heartache: un-
requited hurt much less, but i digress
(resting my head on his skinny shoulder
my eyes shut against the midnight morning
sitting on the brooklyn heights promenade.
he shrugged.

                    i rose

                            only because she'd
phoned an hour since i'd planted my ex-
quisite corpse beneath my permafrosted
childhood dome) as christmas lights flickered i
swallowed mouthfuls of dark stars, letting
go the stream of bodily excuses

bloodletting

letting go, the stream of bodily
excuses telling me i need to go. let's
have some fun—crown of thorns—the body
follows meekly when it's spiked with juices.
traveling through time and starlight, looking
for something to love, with its hooks—
we rocked suddenly and swooned, orbiting
the moon. *weakly mind, weakly. the x-
files'* mulder finally mourns his baby
sister. in my quiesce, no breach of
confidence—only yes's and oh my's—the
history of an evening's joys and—
weakly ooooh i go home—bloodletting
accidentally, proudly after he's gone

4

love cycle

                  has he called? i ask, and my friend
suppresses a laugh

anoint the memory with the meaning of
what isn't
        forgotten:
                how you kissed me
                            ravaging
my mouth
      unsightly, undiscovered
                now brooding on microwave
popcorn
      or the fleshy gyrations of a porno screen: a pas
de deux
    left
        suddenly
              a hand
                   loosened a grip
unfastened.
      (when alone these
             could be mistaken for needs)

choreographed in flawless repetition—
             a pattern to
                 the name

you gave to

what was really

going on:

my illusions:

earnest attempts

at reading your lips

eating

your salty

cum

pleading even

that the stillness never

leave

me.

and it did. as it always

does?

and i quell the urge

to converge

back somehow

onto your bed

now that

your shoulders are   battered

with the brutal mathematics

of consistency

reason for me, then, to retain

the memories

of a few months

and save the plot for another day

another's

way

        of reading abstract symbols

                     the language of

decay as old as

          love itself

               a bitter gamble, this mundane

game

       ever refuses to claim   a winner—

                   i could go

on you see

        forever

           until then—

               let's rewind

to the beginning

5

when i was little (ii)

in santo domingo back then, j—, my mother's boyfriend, who in his early 20s took care of my sister and me while our mother worked in puerto rico, would take us to meetings for christian youth every week, sometimes twice or three times a week. he would play a game with us. we would ask where we were headed that evening, and he would only say, "you'll see." and my heart would flutter. where could it be? i was giddy. imagine my disappointment when we finally wound up in the church courtyard.

every time he would lead us on, and every time i imagined some place different.

in 1981, my mother remarried and was granted a visa to leave for the u.s. my sister and i were not allowed to go with her.

while our mother tried to get us visas, we would get letters from her, and they listed an address in puerto rico. my sister and i joked, she's *really* living on "puerto rico *street*," a few blocks from where we lived in the *ensanche ozama*.

one particularly hard week, my sister and i only had one peso to spend for our allowance. this was never a lot of money, even for a kid, and my sister, the braver of the two, bargained with the bodega. somehow we ate *janiqueque* and orange soda like always.

don p— y doña f—, our landlords, who lived next door, had beautiful trees of *guayaba* and a lot of backyard to play in. i had a stick with a mop i would play with, and pretend it was my grandmother. it kind of looked like her.

once, i had the brilliant idea to only eat *from* the guavas, and yet leave them hanging from the tree. my sister went along with the scheme. we got into so much trouble. doña f— was appalled. we didn't think they would notice.

another time it was *el día de los reyes magos* (day of the epiphany). we had always come close to getting no presents, since i could remember, but we always made it. not this time. it was too late. but in the nick of time, my father came and saved the day. he brought ping pongs, jumping jacks, and i don't remember what else, a bag of miracles. it meant nobody forgot about us.

my sister and i used to get the best toys in the neighborhood, in our mother's topsy-turvy world. she always told me i had many fathers, the better to receive more presents and more love. why settle for one when you can have two, or three? this was our mother's logic. j— looked just like me, but then again so did my father. everyone marveled at how alike i was to j—. i had many fathers. and i had none.

my sister got her visa first. i was the one who stayed behind.

i was eight and a half years old, and was tended by a surrogate family. i got into my first fight (which i won), and remember looking at the moon, my vision blurry. i was a shy kid.

in 1985, when i was allowed entry, my last fifth-grade class in the dominican republic lifted me up on their shoulders, jubilant, as school ended. that was my first moment of happiness.

untitled (dream)

mugging   for   the   camera
he   &   i   wannabe
gangsta   sign   my   lips
his   shaggy   straw
hair   &   i   remembered
something   i   had   lost
something   i   never   had
remembered   never
having   this   memory

begging for quarters

in memoriam
sandra rosado

wearing skyblue button-down   in dark jeans, 14,
ready to go see tim burton's *batman* in manhattan.
i felt so grown—up you were taking me a few days
before you were begging for quarters on flushing
avenue you said wow you look great, and off we
went. gothic skyscrapers, concrete gargoyles and i
was afraid, the first time going out to the movies alone,
with you: shifting eyes, weeks later sitting vibrating, i
didn't understand why you

wore pale yellow, your aunt, my mom talked while i
searched for signs of you as your ponytail turned this
way and that, and again

i was afraid it was something i said, didn't say, didn't
understand, which it was. pale yellow sweater, your
skin even paler, yellower. once you told me how
things were before we came. and—oh! —frankie,
your husband, scary as the scarecrow, rope-a-dope
frame but strong enough to bounce you (i heard the
high-pitched screams—this was nothing you said
because you never talked about it)

instead you talked about living with no heat, no light

in dead of winter, ominous scurrying (*not* bats) so big, you said you could see their eyes.

i searched for yours but they looked away while your aunt talked to my mom who, later, told me what i couldn't—didn't believe—as if heroin was a superhero, your secret identity.

yellow veins throbbing, rigid postures of neglect (your screams cracked like thunder-clouds, as the blows rained down) by day frankie was mild mannered, but i knew now about his dark brow.

(i donated to an aids charity in your name)

you did not die being beaten by your husband you did not die being bitten by rats you did not die begging for quarters at the corner bodega— remember when you asked if i wanted to go beg with you once? a child's simplicity looking everywhere for a sign of the friend who took me to the movies and acted so surprised when i admitted *batman* was scary leaving the theater under the looming towers of babylon.

there you sat, statue come to life, vibrating, clammy skin, yellow eyes. you did not die from your superhero serum. life killed you.

glide with you

for boyd lee dunlop[1]

first glances always lie
say the wise

who know adelaide
will someday stop gliding

and boyd will too
stop gliding with her

inured to the humdrum
moves

of yesterday, cause to
pause and ask her

can i glide with you?

forgetting what the wise already
know

that this gliding will
slow

that adelaide's sore feet
boyd's lead soles

will stop gliding together
then stop gliding at all.

so the wise

but those undisturbed
by the flow

the naïve who believe
in adelaide and boyd

in what moved him
to say, 'the way she walked,

the way she moved. she glided!'

that vision is never gone
that moment isn't

erased by sore feet, sore smiles
that the wise never forget

from reminding us always
come——

what of adelaide, what of her
gliding?

did she ever glide at all?
was boyd a fool

42

as the wise insist, lips drawn into thin
red

eyes drawn to the pair

gliding
'oh god, can i glide with you?'

it's no illusion
to rejoice

to see the beauty of her
what he glimpsed in

that diner
even

knowing that there always
is

an aftermath
but despite

the wise, it may be loving, too, who's
to say there's no sequel

to this love story?
no chapter 2?

who's wise enough to deny that

boyd saw adelaide

gliding

when she was just being
herself

who's wise enough to say that
because of all the heartache

bad breath, sore feet, bad debts—
ruins of

a marriage
(but especially

the bad breath)
who's to say

that because everyone is hopelessly
flawed, ugly

inside since you know
inside is all shit and piss

and
gross

who's to say because
every body is a bag of

bones, a house
of dirty water

because of this
boyd can't say

'oh god, can i glide with you?'

we're bags of bones yet
we glide

alone

when we're not aware
of it, sometimes

when we are
and sometimes

we're lucky
to find a boyd who

turns to us and thinks

'the way she walked, the way she moved.
she glided!'

and asks, 'oh
god can i glide with you?'

raven

alabaster pose as she opens the door. she's
doing her cocaine, but not too much:

she might be working tonight. you see
her brew a cup of coffee, to restrain her

habit. you know her nails are done. she
makes you at home, with her kindness.

on the bathroom mirror, scrawled in wine-
red lipstick: 'your pleasure is our business'

& 'everything went downhill once i started
reading shakespeare.' she says she

doesn't wanna go, she's having too
much fun, so she calls just to see

'cause maybe the john's already asleep
in his hotel room. phone wire wrapped around

her finger: she's right: the john's passed
out. she's calling it a night. goodbye,

thank you, i have to water my plants.

communion

she: photograph

                                        stiff white dress, squint
                                        in sunlight

bright stoop steps

                        i received:
                                        pillow of
my tongue

                stolen afternoon
                count my bones

                                                bruise

afternoon
                we are
                more beautiful than photographs

sweet whiteness on the tongue

                                        {and i am a woman singing}

6

gay chat room: found poem

>sigh< are there any average looking tops in nyc or are they all hot
        and hung?
if you get a hot one then everyone wants him, and i just don't want to
        share!
(well, ok, maybe on fridays...)

i found queens to be the borough with the hottest trolls

<that made me a few more fans>

you had no fans to begin with.

u have pets that love u

they don't suck my dick, though.

true but they could be trained

no suckie, no worth it

(i tried my best not to go down that road)
but i feel the evil rising in me tonight

i just ignored it
and as for the evil, let it out!
get it out of your system!

i got no one to unload on

that's everyone's problem here tonight.

visiting ny, any sex clubs?

lol

yeah, hooters

more like cock and balls

my club is a real hoot
depends on how good u lick it

where is heaven located?[2]

i've had some practice.

right between my legs

who's looking to shoot a huge load

hell
we are talking about *heaven*

who's gonna open wide and say ahhh?

so bring your tongue and kneepads over here
(setting myself up for a putdown)

are you talking to me?

yup

think again

go yankees

(ehhh, pretty mild turndown)

try bossman, he likes to service

go diamondbacks

i like losers with no profiles

friday the 13th

has it ever happened to you
that sudden inexplicable

recoil
from the precipice—

you learn and you learn and you
loosen your tongue

toward a stranger whose
own tastes as warm as

rhubarb pie.

what they call
love, sometimes

a pattern
a tapestry.

you both move on
like a still photo in

late afternoon rain
and you think spring

is the only time

there is. but summer comes

like a thief
he steals all

your belongings.
you are naked

and free at the beach

nocturnes

i.

there's no word for it besides
where would you stand
before lightning strikes—

inside a cab shivering
the rain's sharp strings
sizzle from your skin.

you laugh, so you fall
from the permanent wind.
your shoes are untied

the bed unmade—the sky
turns violent.

ii.

the entire city scrapes
your feet encased
in its glassy temper.

your musician's ear like a
stranger's
echoing

iii.
'we are different beings
for different things'
and the fire in his palms...

'we are different beings
for different things, some
given, some taken back

against grey skies
leaden with irony'

ex soliloquy #4

o is this what i want as the stairs
seem to narrow like your waist

running down cabs in the rainy a.m.
(getting to work on time i should say)

let me go and we're off in separate ways

ready to embark on the voyage of adam's
apple, solar plexus

and we pray

listening to dots and sparkles
staticky interim

where i stay, looking down a
gorgeous display

of affection, a sunk ship
bottled and precious

violin sex

the gold medal around his neck
flecks of his eyes

shards of goldenrod
crayola smile

mirrored thing so lovely
you tell me

lines of cocaine as white
as your eyes

envisioning

the ecstasy of me, this room, this
meeting of bone muscle skin

a performance you want to attend
the sex so damn good you want it all

over again, and when it's done
the perfect cupid's bow of your lips

gives me that expensive kiss

and the laugh track surrounding
us when the fantasy is

done, never to behold

the measures of reality
inexact and slightly

hypocritical—small
lies of yesterday morning

when repeating the scene
you realize how

he said, your hands touching me
like a master handles his violin.

the somnambulist

ready for bed and all its seasons
i grab your wrists

to stop you from
bolting. you break free

trample
downstairs

bump into kitchen
table (the floor's

math takes some
getting used to)

huge cylinders of you, an
archipelago

deluged in
the smell of my armpit.

american sign language

there's nothing about you i don't like:
sunset, glistening fingers.
of course, you say, now give up this.

the waiter pours coffee for one.
how we sat, waiting for words
(there's nothing about you I don't like)

we had breakfast and pretended
wherever we sat, the sunrise. but
of course you say, now give up this

walking on the beach of my back as
softness turned to hunger, silence—
there's nothing about me you don't like—

your face slips by me in the shower
when i'm only being myself, getting clean—
of course, you say, now give up this.

at blue & gold, the east village dive bar
afterwards, signing the words, whistling
there's nothing about me you don't like.
of course, i say, now give this up.

tired of finding

the territorial arc of my arms
wrapped around you like a damp

down comforter. not even warm
much less—comfortable

tell me when does this language describe

an actual love affair—you choose
and you lose your metaphors

winding down a glass spiral staircase:

the steps i take along a park fence
before meeting you at your place—

let's not continue this, i want so much
more than to be jealous of your pain.

'i want to want you all to myself' and
i inhale as i call

a block away from your home holding
a six pack of beer

trying to see if you're there

your voice silent over the line because
i wish it so.

the trojan horse

under azure sky wrapped in
cellophane, in the snowbird
mountains, lost

without a companion.
love is a tricycle, the buddhist
version of a triangle. picture

the rustle of yellow leaves
backed by pink and red rock
and a sky bluer than that.

my friend on the other side
whose tongue I've tasted in every
vernacular, shuffles his eyes

toward mine like a cat pounces
on top of its prey, poised to play
a little game—

let's be friends again, the wind
whispers longingly. altitude under
my feet, hiking among mormons

praying in the light of day. he
tastes like you, sexy beard
stubble, red-eyed, gorgeous.

he has nothing to say of his fears.
only the skin we're in allows
me to say: the light passes through

the hallway—i dream of a sky marred
by two ravens flying in unison. you,
my friend on the other side of the atlantic

coasting on pride and quickness—
you fly away, already rearranged
your life assumes the change in season

acknowledgments

Evie Shockley
Sven Davisson
Walter Holland
Julia Bouwsma
Emanuel Xavier
Carlos Ulises Decena
Rigoberto González
Seth Parker Woods
Dawn Heather Bossman
Malado Francine Baldwin-Tejeda
Jesse Dancy
Mark Boulos
Beck Feibelman
Erwan Augoyard
Pia Deas
Lynda Kong
Neil DiMaio
Nicolette Englert
Mark Trushkowsky
Joshua Carr
Alvina
Scott Withey
Keelyn Bradley
Ian Lague
Nayef Homsi
Rob Calentine
Steven Harris

A. J. Fung
David Schultz
Wil Edgar
Daniel Hart
Brian Fuss
Aden Ardennes
Shane O'Brien

... and to all the men & boys who shall remain nameless but not faceless in my mind's eye, and even those i can't recall right now ... who i've loved & who loved me ... for an hour, a night, a season, or a lifetime

& Brian Paul

notes

1   based on dan barry's new york times article, 9 december 2011, on boyd lee dunlop, a jazz pianist who recounts his youthful romance with adelaide and his eventual redemption, being rediscovered in a nursing home in buffalo, ny.

2   heaven was a gay nightclub in chelsea, popular when the diamondbacks won the world series in 2001.

Printed in the USA
CPSIA information can be obtained
at www.ICGtesting.com
LVHW05074028Q823
756385LV00087B/644